The Ultimate Guide to
Property Insurance Claims
in the UK

Five Deadly Sins That Can Destroy Your Insurance Claim
(Avoid them and you stand a good chance of winning!)

First Edi...

STEVE L∴∴∴∷

First published in 2015 by The Claims Desk
9 Birkbeck Road, London NW7 4BP United Kingdom

info@theclaimsdesk.co.uk
www.theclaimsdesk.co.uk

ISBN 978-1-78280-660-8

The right of Steve Lazarus to be identified as the author of this work has been asserted in accordance with sections 77 and 78 of the Copyright Designs and Patents Act 1988.

A CIP catalogue record for this book is available from the British Library.

Dedication

To my beautiful wife Soli: who didn't bat an eyelid 11 years ago when I told her I was quitting my day job and decent regular income to set up The Claims Desk... with no clients and no sign of a pay cheque. She has supported me every single step of the way and is now very much an integral part of what we have achieved at The Claims Desk. She sustains me when things are tough and is also an incredible Mum. I love her dearly.

To my son David: I want you to know that you are an amazing handsome young man, with a sensitive soul and a sharp wit. You have so much to offer and you can achieve wonderful things. Remember, "The best things in life are free" and that I love you very much.

To my daughter Rosie: You are beautiful, intelligent and single minded, and I have no doubt you will go on to excel in whatever you choose in life. The world is your oyster and I know that you will absorb every new experience that awaits you. Life is full of amazing opportunities and I am sure you will grab them gleefully. I love you loads.

To my dad Alan: I have always looked up to you and you have always been my role model for hard work, ethics and meticulous preparation for everything in life. Thank you for your love, support and friendship over the years. I am very proud of you and all your amazing achievements. COYS.

To my mum Marylin: Sometimes words just fail me. You are an incredible lady. You are a force of nature and a shining beacon to everyone in our family and to anyone who has ever come into contact with you. Your love and support for me and all your family is incredible and I want you to know I love you and appreciate all you have done for me over the years.

To my sister Lorraine: Last but by no means least. My beautiful sister. Life has been terribly cruel to you I know, but you have borne your troubles with dignity, and the love for your family never fails to shine through. You always liven up a room and keep us honest and on our toes, and the purity of your soul is there for all to see. I love you dearly and pray life will get a little easier for you.

Contents

If you can answer YES to these six questions, we may be the insurance claims experts for YOU

1. Do you have damage to your residential or commercial property, expected to cost at least £5,000 to repair or replace?

2. Was the damage caused by fire, theft, flood, storm, subsidence or malicious damage?

3. Was the damage 'fortuitous' – in other words, unforeseen?

4. Do you believe you have a current insurance policy in place that you think should cover you for this damage?

5. Have you reported the damage to your insurance company or broker within the stipulated time period set out in your policy?

6. Have you only just discovered or suffered the damage?

If you can answer YES to all of these questions, then call us NOW on 0208 906 0098/07782 195455

About The Claims Desk
Fewer cases for us
= More time for <u>YOU</u>

Not all loss assessors are the same. Indeed we at The Claims Desk are 'different'.

We don't handle every type of claim under the sun. We don't deal with motor claims. We don't deal with injury claims. We don't deal with professional indemnity claims. There are various other categories of claim we also don't handle. But we DO deal with property claims, without needing to chase for them. Why? Because our reputation in this field means that people come to us.

By dealing with fewer claims, we have more time to deal with your claim thoroughly to achieve the best results.

Steve Lazarus has been dealing with property insurance claims since 1990. He set up and has been Director of The Claims Desk since 2004. All of our clients have been referred to us by former satisfied clients and by other professionals in the property and insurance industry.

Sometimes, the best advice you can be given when you think you have a valid insurance claim is that you do NOT have a winnable case. When that is the case, we will be honest enough to tell you. We will also tell you if we feel you can deal with the claim yourself.

But if your case passes our test and we accept you as a client, you will receive close personal attention. We will represent you tenaciously but fairly, whilst keeping you up to date on all relevant matters.

We will explain all fees and costs to you fully before we start working on your case.

Why THIS Book?

I wrote this book because, if you are like most people and business owners, this is probably the first time you will have suffered significant damage to your home or business and you will have lots of questions.

You may have spoken to your insurance company or broker and be unsure about the questions you are being asked, or find it hard to understand the process and the purpose of all the different suppliers being potentially foisted upon you.

Your insurer may even have told you that they cannot help and that your claim is not covered. Frustratingly, they may tell you that they can't get anyone out to see you for weeks. This is bad news if your home is badly damaged and you need alternative accommodation, or if your business has had to close temporarily and your cash-flow is affected.

You may have started to make enquiries into loss assessors, but not found any that provide useful information about how to find the right one to handle your particular claim.

Most of the ads say, "Hire me – no-win, no-fee" and say that they will "care for you" or "We are aggressive". This is completely meaningless as this is surely the minimum you require from an effective loss assessor.

So, I have written this book for YOU.

Sit down quietly at home and have a good read on your own without any pressure or distraction. Do this BEFORE you hire a loss assessor and BEFORE you make any further contact with your insurance company and/or their loss adjuster. You may find that you don't even need a loss assessor to help with your claim.

Crucial Definitions

Loss adjuster – Insurance claims expert who acts for and on behalf of the insurance company and is paid by them to deal with your claim. Supposed to be impartial but is not!

Loss assessor – Insurance claims expert who acts exclusively for YOU, the claimant, and MUST be authorised and regulated by the FCA.

Financial Conduct Authority – Regulator of the financial services industry in the UK, with the aim of protecting YOU the consumer.

Insurer/underwriter – Insurance company providing you with the cover you need.

Insured perils – Fire, theft, flood, storm and escape of water. All the various events you want to be insured against.

Insurance broker – Agent who scours the market for you and tries to find the most suitable insurance cover for you.

Myths and Truths

Myths you may have heard from friends, neighbours and relatives (and other well-intentioned folk)

Frequently I hear people say things that sound like they should be true and accurate but in fact have no bearing on reality whatsoever. Here are some myths that must be dispelled before we go any further.

Myth 1
If you write to your insurance company and are reasonable, they will make you a reasonable settlement offer in return.

Truth 1
From the outset you need to appreciate that insurers have totally different vested interests to you.

They are invariably £multi-million/£billion businesses and conglomerates which have stakeholders to consider such as shareholders and pension funds. So if they can save a buck here and there they will do so. Their share price is sacrosanct.

Meanwhile all you want is to be put back in the position you were in before you suffered your loss. This, after all, is what insurance is for.

However, your idea of what is 'reasonable' does not always reflect the view of your insurer. To muddy the waters even further, you may not even know what is classified as 'reasonable', as you may not know what you are entitled to claim. And insurers don't go out of their way to tell you.

You end up in a position of not knowing what you don't know, and insurers are happy for that to remain the position for as long as possible.

When it comes to your claim, insurers have the upper hand. Consider this - they wrote the policy and they appoint experts to act for them to settle your claim. And they don't tell you the rules of the game. So what chance do you have of getting a reasonable settlement? The most unreasonable thing they do is not giving you a clue about what is 'reasonable'…

Myth 2
Insurance company loss adjusters are totally impartial.

Truth 2
In theory a chartered loss adjuster is supposed to be impartial and deal with your claim fairly. The dictionary definition of 'impartial' is 'unbiased, unprejudiced, neutral, non-partisan, and non-discriminatory'.

In my experience this is certainly not the case. After all, it's insurance companies which pay the loss adjuster's fees. Insurance companies audit the loss adjuster's files. Insurance companies measure key performance indicators (KPIs) such as the number of claims declined; the savings on claims (known in the trade as 'leakage' – kind of an ironic term if your declined claim is for flood damage); the number of claims referred to fraud investigators; and the number of claims where insurers' preferred suppliers are used. Are you getting the picture?

The loss adjuster will create a detailed written report for the insurance company. This contains a significant amount of detail about you, your home or your business and all of the circumstances surrounding your claim. In this report, they will make recommendations to your insurer about how your claim should be dealt with. They will give an opinion about whether your claim is valid or whether further enquiries are required. This whole report is classified as privileged information and therefore you are not allowed access to it.

Does this sound 'impartial' to you?

Myth 3
All loss assessors have the same competencies and skills.

Truth 3
Loss assessors come in all shapes and sizes and as with any profession there are many to choose from. So you need to choose carefully.

A loss assessor does not have to be qualified, but does have to be authorised and regulated by the Financial Conduct Authority. This does not provide an indicator of competency. It simply means that you should be covered if you receive poor advice. If you choose the right loss assessor it doesn't need to get to that stage.

So how do you go about choosing the right loss assessor? Here are various factors to consider:

• A truly excellent loss assessor will have many years' experience dealing with a wide variety of claims and should be more than willing to sit down and discuss the merits of your claim before taking your instruction.

- Check to see if the loss assessor has good current client testimonials.

- Speak to clients who have used the loss assessor before.

- Has the loss assessor written technical papers and does he/she speak on topics and network widely?

- Is the loss assessor respected in his/her local community, and does he/she have extensive contacts within the insurance and associated industry?

You see, anyone can call themselves a loss assessor, but the truth is that there are very few who are technically excellent, organised and have the people and management skills to deal with all the various parties involved in your claim.

A loss assessor must keep a clear head at all times, and manage your expectations. Don't sign up to the first one who promises the earth. All that glitters is not gold!

Myth 4
'New for old' means 'New for old'

Truth 4
Many years ago, if you had a claim, the insurance company would settle it by paying you an 'indemnity'. This was basically the replacement cost of the items, less an amount for wear and tear and depreciation to reflect the age and condition of the items.

Over the years and as market trends dictated, insurers improved their policies and started to offer what we now know as 'new for old'. This simply means that when you claim for something that is a few years old, insurers should pay you the current replacement cost or supply the nearest current equivalent.

However, there are items that many household policies will not pay out as 'new for old', such as clothing and linen. Sometimes insurers won't pay you 'new for old' if you don't actually replace the item.

Other times, insurers won't pay you 'new for old' if you are under-insured. This in itself is a potential minefield and a common area of dispute – see Deadly Sin 2.

Myth 5
Insurance companies treat their customers fairly and care about you.

Truth 5
The Financial Conduct Authority, which authorises and regulates insurance companies in the UK, expects customers' interests to be at the heart of how insurers conduct their business. This is known at TCF (Treating Customers Fairly).

"Customers can expect to get financial services and products that meet their needs from firms that they can trust. Meeting customers' fair and reasonable expectations should be the responsibility of firms, not that of the regulator." (Extract from the FCA website, last modified 3 March 2015)

We've all seen insurers' glossy ads in the media. They promise the earth, with snappy slogans, smart logos and voiceovers and endorsements by famous actors and celebrities.

Yet in 2013/14 the FOS (Financial Ombudsman Service) received over 800,000 enquiries for all sectors. 38,000 cases were considered in detail by the ombudsman, of which 58% were found in favour of the complainant (Source: FOS complaints data). That's an awful lot of cases that were contested by insurers and financial services companies, only to be found in favour of YOU the policyholder. The data for 2014 shows a similar picture.

So just imagine you have made a claim for a fire or a theft or a flood. You are already seriously stressed and out of pocket. And then along comes your insurance company to decline your claim, slash its value, or simply to treat you shabbily. You then have to go through a formal complaints process with them before you can even take your claim to the FOS. They then take several months to arrive at a decision, as they cannot cope with their volume of complaints. And then on top of all that, you have only around a 50% chance of winning your claim.

Is that treating you fairly?

NOTES

Tricky Insurance Companies and Loss Adjusters

I am fed up with insurance companies taking advantage of people before they have had a chance to take professional advice from a loss assessor. All too often, I have been made aware that the insurance company and their loss adjusters will actually put claimants off instructing a loss assessor. They will say things like, "Why do you need to appoint one? We will deal with this for you" or, "You know they charge and that you will have to pay for it".

Only a few weeks ago a client approached me, as she wasn't at all happy with the way her insurance company was treating her and dealing with her claim for water damage.

To cut a very long story short, her insurers offered her circa £12,000 to repair the damage, having first butchered her lovely home with drying and temporary repairs. All the while she had to continue to live in the house. When she notified her insurers that she was instructing The Claims Desk to deal with the claim for her, they had the nerve to tell her in an email that all we would do would be to inflate the claim and slow down the claims process. Indeed, they wrote to me and said they would not increase the offer because we were now instructed. How petty. How ignorant.

As it turns out, we reviewed the claim, and following a meeting with the insurer's surveyor the claim was finally agreed at around £22,000. It was clear they had not considered the full scope of the works, nor had they advised our client that she could in fact claim for certain other elements she had not even considered. So much for treating the customer fairly.

Insurance companies love to use fear to dissuade people from getting good sound advice, which is odd. They instruct a claims expert to look after THEIR interests, so you should at least have the chance to consider YOUR options, don't you think?

Guess what? You may not need a loss assessor to represent you, but you should at least know who and what is out there for you and understand the system and what you are up against. The insurance company doesn't truly care about you despite their glossy brochures and expensive celebrity endorsed ads. They don't know you.

The loss adjuster's main focus is to get the claim settled and off his desk, so he can get his fees in and his bonus sorted. How do I know – I've been there, done it and got the t-shirt.

Here are some other tactics some (not all) insurance companies use, simply to wear you down in the hope you will go away:

1. **Deliberate delay.** They know you are up against it in terms of time, money and knowledge. So by dragging out the entire process, they hope you will simply give up in exasperation and go away quietly. Regrettably many do.

2. **Request unnecessary information.** Insurance companies are of course entitled to require you to provide reasonable information to enable them to deal with your claim. Often though, the amount of information requested is spurious and simply designed to send you on a wild goose chase so that they

can take longer to do nothing and sit on your money.

3. **Dispute facts.** I frequently meet loss adjusters who know everything about everything and will say black is white without any foundation or verification, simply to avoid paying a claim. Or they will blind you with science in the hope you will shrug your shoulders and say, "I guess they must be right then". They are not always correct. They are often wrong.

4. **Misrepresent insurance benefits.** Time and again, the loss adjuster will not tell you what you are actually covered for or what you may be able to claim for under the terms of the policy. If you don't mention it, neither will they. It's not their role to help you present your claim, even though they are claims experts. After all, they are paid by insurers.

5. **Acting like your friend and making false promises.** 'Smiling assassins'. When I first started out over 25 years ago, loss adjusters were known in the industry as 'smiling assassins'. They would smile when they met you and promise you the world. Then they would return to their office, check the small print and find a reason not pay the claim or to reduce the value of the claim.

I have written this book for YOU. To empower YOU.

You need to know the processes that insurers employ. You need to know the motivation of loss adjusters. You need to know that not all loss assessors are the same despite some making outrageous promises.

It is only right and proper too that you are advised when you don't have a valid claim, so that your precious time isn't wasted and your expectations raised only to be shattered.

The Claims Desk only handles legitimate claims for genuine claimants. We make no false promises of quick cash for your suffering. That's not what we are about.

NOTES

The Five Deadly Sins that can Wreck Your Claim

1. You fail to disclose to your insurers some 'material fact' they rely on when they decide whether or not to insure you, or on what terms to insure you.

There are so many examples of what is commonly called 'material non-disclosure'.

An insurance policy is a legally binding contract between you and the insurance company. It is a very special type of contract known as a 'Contract of the Utmost Good Faith'. This is because, with a contract when you buy something like a pair of trainers in a shop, you can actually see and touch the product you are buying. However, with insurance there is nothing to see apart from the contract, and nothing actually happens until you need to make a claim. Therefore, insurers are relying on you to answer all their questions accurately and honestly at the time you buy the policy. AND – very importantly – that information must be accurate and honest at each renewal and across the lifetime of the policy.

Typically, when you take out a policy, insurers will ask a whole host of questions about you, your occupation, your property, its construction, how you use the property etc. Now, if the questions are all clear and you answer them all honestly and accurately to the best of your ability, then when you come to make a claim you should not have any problems.

But this area is fraught with difficulty. Was the question reasonable, was it answered accurately, is it relevant to the claim, did your answer have a bearing on whether insurers decided to insure you or not? The list of imponderables goes on and on.

However, the golden rule has to be: you must ALWAYS read the small print. Sorry about that, as even by the standards of most small print, insurance policy wording is less than riveting and really does go on a bit.

But if you read it with the attitude that doing so could potentially be saving you thousands of pounds, then that can make it as compelling as a good detective story.

So, this means looking in detail at your proposal form, at the statement of fact sent to you, and at your policy booklet. Make sure you are 100% happy with what you have submitted, AND the cover you have been offered and agreed to.

If there is any doubt, you MUST speak to your insurers to clarify. You cannot afford to run any risk of insurers not meeting their obligation to pay your valid claim when the time comes – and it will come!

Tip – if in doubt, employ the services of a good insurance broker, whose job it is to find you the best insurance cover at the most competitive rate.

All good experienced loss assessors should be able to point you in the right direction. Brokers have different skill sets. Some are good at finding the best commercial insurance for blocks of flats, whilst others are good at high net worth residential properties, and yet others are good at Chinese restaurants. The point here is, as with everything in life, there is an expert out there who can specifically help you.

Don't take a chance, don't be cheap, and make sure you know exactly what you are buying!

Don't give insurers an excuse not to pay your claim because you didn't pay attention at the beginning. You will sorely regret it later.

At the time of writing, royal assent has been given to the **Insurance Act 2015**, which is due to come into force in August 2016. This time-gap is to allow brokers and insurers ample time to update their paperwork and policies to facilitate the Act's new measures.

In practical terms there are three main areas you will need to be aware of. The one we are interested in here is 'The Duty of Fair Presentation'. This will impose on you the duty to make a disclosure to insurers of a) every material circumstance you know or ought to know and b) sufficient information to put a prudent insurer on notice that they need to make further enquiries for the purpose of revealing those material circumstances.

'Material circumstances' are any circumstances that would influence the judgment of a prudent insurer in determining whether to insure you and if so on what terms.

You cannot take the view, "Don't ask, don't tell", as any material circumstances which are suspected or should have been known will have to be disclosed.

If you breach this duty, either deliberately or recklessly, insurers may be able to avoid the contract (i.e. treat it as if it never happened), demand a higher premium or change the terms retrospectively.

2. Your insurer says that you are 'under-insured'

This is a neat trick that insurers and their loss adjusters keep up their sleeves as a typical 'go to' clause to reduce your claim settlement and sometimes even avoid your claim and/or your policy altogether.

When you take out an insurance policy, you are told you have a duty to insure your contents, stock and buildings etc. for the full replacement value. So, for example, you insure the contents of your home for, say, £50,000 and your home burns down. Could you replace all your contents for £50,000? If you can, then in simple terms you are 'adequately insured'. If you can't, then you may well have a problem.

You see, it is a condition of your policy that you insure for the full replacement value AND that you continue to do so throughout the life of your policy. It's in the infamous 'small print'. The reason is as follows. You are expecting insurers to insure you for the full value of all your contents and in return they calculate a premium based on this value. Therefore, if you are not paying them sufficient premium they will contend that they should not be covering you for the full replacement value. Follow?

Now, every insurance company is different. They will have different wording and different in-house policies (that of course you never get to see). Their tolerance levels will vary, although again you won't be made aware of these. Broadly speaking they can penalise you in one of several ways, depending often on how much you are under-insured.

- They may settle your claim, but instead of getting the 'new for old' value, they will give you an amount less wear and tear and depreciation (known as indemnity).

- They can give you a percentage of the agreed value of your claim (known as average). So, if you are underinsured by say 30%, they will reduce your claim by 30%.

- If you are really badly underinsured, they can 'avoid' your policy altogether. This means that they will cancel your policy from the date you took it out, and then of course you can't claim at all! Your policy never existed!

These are just a few of the responses you may come up against. So you need to be aware of this common ploy, and of course think carefully about counter arguments that can be employed against them.

It's an awful feeling to be told you are underinsured and that you will only be getting a fraction of what you are claiming, or that you can't claim at all. I have seen this all too often.

So, these first two deadly sins show you just how technical insurance claims can be. They are seldom plain sailing. And there are three more to consider...

3. Lack of Proof

Most, if not all, insurance policies will require you to produce some form of proof of ownership. This is especially relevant when you need to make a claim for the theft of contents from your home or stock/contents from your office. This requirement will be one of the many 'claim conditions' that your insurance company will require you to comply with – sometimes strictly and to the letter.

As I have said before, every policy is different and that is what makes dealing with claims so complex. There are literally thousands of policies on the market and each one is worded slightly differently. However, common to all of them will be an insistence that you produce for them or their loss adjusters some 'proof of ownership' (POO!) for the item or items you are claiming.

The reason for this of course is to prove that you had the item in the first place. Insurers are a cynical bunch and if you can't produce a receipt, what else are they to assume, other than you never had the item in the first place.

Insurers may be satisfied with a purchase receipt or a bank/credit card statement. Sometimes a box, an operator's manual or photo of the item may suffice. But you need to show them all the evidence and proof they can reasonably request if you are to satisfy this requirement.

Sometimes for jewellery items they can insist on a valuation made within the last 12 months! Have you got yours?

What do you do if all your records are destroyed in a fire and are not backed up anywhere?

If you fail to comply – and let's face it, who keeps all their receipts – then you may well come unstuck for part or all of your claim.

Tip: Keep a folder of all your purchase receipts and manuals etc. for items with an individual value greater than say £100.

Take photos of each room in your home to capture key items such as TVs and computers. Do this annually so you are always up to date.

Make sure you have all jewellery items worth over £1000 valued every few years – unless your policy is stricter than this – and keep this with your file. This may sound like a bit of a chore but, believe me, it may be the difference between a successful claim and a train wreck.

4. Misrepresenting/overstating your claim

Simply put, "DON'T DO IT!" It may be tempting. You will hear others say "Insurers deserve it" or "You've been paying premiums for years, so why not?" or "It's not theft – they can afford it".

WRONG! It IS theft! However tempting it may be to add a few things to your claim or increase the value unrealistically, please don't do it.

First off, it is fraud and all insurance policies have a fraud condition that basically says that if they can show that your claim is in any way fraudulent they will not pay your claim. It's obvious isn't it? But many people fall foul of this. Some make up the whole claim and some simply exaggerate it. Insurers may also prosecute you and you will almost certainly be blacklisted and never get insurance again. Never get insurance again – think about the implications of that…

Now I should point out that there are some – not many, but there are some – unscrupulous loss assessors out there. They will either endorse the fraudulent actions of their client or indeed positively encourage it by embellishing the facts of a claim or by adding items that were never stolen.

Warning:– Do not do it. Do not think about it. Do not be tempted.

We will never work for a client where we believe that they have acted improperly or in a fraudulent manner. Others might, but we will not and we will not be shy in telling you.

However, we will defend our clients against false or improper allegations where we see it. We have done so successfully in the past. But if any evidence of impropriety comes to light and is justified against a client, then I am afraid it is "au revoir". We have an excellent reputation in the market place for being firm but fair and we will not under any circumstances do anything to jeopardize our standing or indeed our FCA registration. You should not expect us to.

Under the new **Insurance Act 2015**, insurers will be able to treat the contract as having been terminated from the date of the fraudulent act and need not return any premiums. The insurer will not be liable for the claim AND will be able to recover any payments made.

5. Breach of Warranty

I could write a whole other book under this heading but the intention here is simply to alert you to this potential minefield.

In basic terms, a warranty is a clause in an insurance policy that states, "You must do this" or "You must not do that". Now, the nature of these often very specific instructions will vary from risk to risk, insurer to insurer and policy to policy.

Further, there are different types of warranty. There are those warranties that must be complied with in order for your policy to even be valid, or else insurers would not have insured you. Then there are those warranties that you must comply with at specific times and for specific events, and if you don't, then insurers can refuse to deal with your claim.

To make matters even more complicated – and this is an area subject to much discussion, debate, internal underwriting and common law – there is the issue of 'materialism'. In other words, was your breach of a warranty 'material' to the loss or damage you are claiming, or was the breach simply 'technical'?

Now, I never set out in this book to get all techie with you, but the nature of an insurance policy – which is, after all, a legally binding contract between you and your insurer – inevitably means that I have to get a little bit techie to make the point.

So, let me give you a classic common example of how a simple breach of warranty can affect your otherwise valid claim.

A lot of household policies will have a warranty in them that will state that you must have certain locks on external doors and accessible windows, and that these locks must be put into operation whenever you leave the house unoccupied or go to bed at night.

Now, what if **you think** you have all of these locks and pop out to the shops for an hour, securing the house before you leave. When you get back, your house has been burgled and it seems the intruders got in by forcing the rear patio doors. You report the claim to your insurers and they instruct their loss adjuster to deal with the claim for them.

The loss adjuster turns up and inspects the locks to make sure you comply. But, lo and behold, it is found that although the lock on the patio door complied with the warranty, the lock on the front door didn't. Now, strictly speaking, this should not be 'material', as this is not how the thieves got in. But insurers may say, "Ah well, had we known you had the wrong locks on your front door we would not have insured you in the first place", and proceed to kick your claim into touch.

What if there was no sign of forced entry, but you swear blind that you locked all the doors and windows before you went out? Do you think it will be easy to get the insurance company to believe that you complied with the warranty? Do you think they will play hardball with you?

What if the intruders got in through a window that you didn't feel in your wildest dreams was accessible to anyone other than Superman, and so you didn't have a lock fitted? Is that now a 'material' breach of the security warranty? Will your insurers 'repudiate' your claim? There are way too many variables to discuss them all here. Suffice to say, the whole area of policy warranty is hotly debated and contested, and in my many years' experience is the most common excuse for insurers to avoid paying out on an otherwise valid claim.

All too often I see clients who are 100% genuine, who have suffered a genuine loss or damage, but who come unstuck for a completely innocent breach of a warranty. They either missed the small print, misinterpreted the small print, or sometimes the small print was not made clear to them at the point of sale. This latter point raises the whole area of mis-selling, which itself can be hugely stressful for you.

Having said all this, the **Insurance Act 2015** (which takes effect in August 2016) says that breaches of warranty that are irrelevant to the loss that occurs will no longer discharge insurers from liability.

So, for example, I have a claim at present where an industrial unit has burnt down. There is a warranty that states my client must have an alarm, but they didn't have the specified type. However, the lack of the correct alarm clearly has no relevance to the fire and insurers cannot therefore decline the claim on this basis.

Warranties will still exist under the Act, but will be harder to create and will be more limited in scope. Furthermore, representations that you make in your proposal form cannot be made into warranties. Proposal forms and policy wordings will have to be revised to reflect this.

I foresee many contentious issues in this highly complex area until the law is tested in the courts and settles down.

The point I wish you to take from these five deadly sins is not that they are exhaustive. They most certainly are not. There are many other sins. Neither have I covered all the technicalities for each of them. I have not. My intention here is simply to shine a little light on some of the key areas where, if you are not very careful indeed, you may well come horribly unstuck in your hour of need – even innocently.

Big Tip: Always read the small print, as boring as it seems. If in doubt ask your insurer what it means.

6. Bonus Sin – Impatience

'Patience is bitter but its fruits are sweet' Jean-Jacques Rousseau

I don't know about you, but I can be very impatient when I want something. Insurance claims are no exception. It's likely that you know you are correct. You know you have a valid claim and you know that you have provided your insurer with everything they have asked for and more. You simply want them to accept your claim so you can get on with your life.

But, and this is a big but... insurers don't play by your rules. They play by their own. Despite all their promises and marketing puffs, they have zero intention of paying your claim unless they are totally satisfied that your claim is valid and they have exhausted all their enquiries – many which may be totally spurious – AND performed every stalling tactic in the book.

It is hugely frustrating and you need the patience of a saint. Not only will insurers delay dealing with your claim through the sheer volume of enquiries they make, but there will be in-built delays inside their claims handling processes, and within the multitude of suppliers they involve too.

Further, many insurers often employ inexperienced, low grade or incompetent staff, and certainly they employ staff who will never have seen a real claim up close and personal in their lives.

So they cannot empathise with your suffering, have no desire to speed up the process and have little technical hands-on knowledge.

This 'perfect storm' frequently leads to enormous stress and frustration on your part. Not only have you suffered loss or damage, but now you are having your guts ripped out while you are put through the emotional ringer.

Patience is a virtue and you need to keep calm, collected and organised, and then the fruits of your efforts will be rightfully yours.

NOTES

The Insurance Company Will Stop at Nothing to Destroy Your Claim!

This is not always true, but there are so many examples of insurers digging their heels in and seeking to rely on small print to avoid paying your claim.

Now, we all know that fraud is not uncommon in the insurance claims arena and that it costs the industry (and you and I) £millions. But the genuine policyholder who has suffered a terrible fire, flood or theft should not be made to suffer the indignity of a full blown investigation on a whim when insurers and their loss adjusters have a hunch or suspicion that the claim is not quite right.

Insurers need detailed evidence of wrongdoing before they can make accusations of fraud, but all too often we see detailed statements having been taken from a client, as if to indicate that the insurer doesn't believe their client and is trying to catch them out.

We see credit and other background checks done, sometimes without the claimant's consent.

We see fraud teams appointed to dig around or private investigators instructed.

If you have suffered a genuine loss or damage, just imagine how it feels to be investigated at the same time as having to deal with the aftermath of a claim, whilst trying to get your life back in order. Often, I have clients in tears in front of me, on the verge of a breakdown. It's not pleasant.

Now I am totally set against the fraudster – as I have indicated earlier – and would never act for or be associated with one. However, we need to take a reasonable and rational approach to claims. Not all claims are straightforward and often there is more than one possible explanation and interpretation for a set of circumstances. It is all a question of reasonableness.

Insurers in this country have a duty to Treat Customers Fairly. We do not see this enough, either in their policy interpretation or claims handling processes.

NOTES

What About YOUR Claim?

OK, so now you are hopefully a bit more prepared and informed when it comes to making a successful property insurance claim. What have you learned?

• You have a clear view on the role of the insurer, the loss adjuster and the loss assessor, so that you can call on appropriate help if you need it.

• You know that insurance is necessary, insurance is good, and insurance can be your friend... BUT you now know that it's all a bit of a game of cat and mouse.

• You now know the most common myths surrounding insurance claims and the truth that lies behind them.

• You know the ~~five~~ six deadly sins when making a claim and how to avoid them.

• You know the motives of the loss adjuster. And you know that a loss assessor is very different to a loss adjuster...

• You know that honesty is ALWAYS the best policy.

Armed with all that knowledge, you as David can now take on the Goliath of the insurance companies and, I reckon, now stand a better chance of a fair fight and a correct outcome. And if you need someone to be alongside you in your fight, then my details are listed at the end of this book... **Good luck with your claim...**

Appendix
The Claims Desk:
Our Cases and Settlements

Here are some examples of claims that The Claims Desk has handled. It is of course important to recognise that each case is different and these in no way represent what your claim is worth or indeed the merits of YOUR case.

We are also honest enough to say that we do not win every claim – but we certainly settle the vast majority, with results that often exceed our clients' expectations. Our clients are frequently delighted with the results we achieve and the service we provide, and you can see dozens of testimonials on our website, *www.theclaimsdesk.co.uk*. So, here are some of our results:-

Case 1
£79,000 settlement achieved with insurers who initially only offered £46,600.

We were instructed – on the anonymous recommendation of a loss adjuster, who was not happy with the way he felt this claimant was being treated by insurers – to review and renegotiate a settlement put forward by the insurance company.

Our client's large detached house – that he had built himself – was damaged substantially by water, following a burst tank. His insurers sent round their own surveyors and contractors to prepare a schedule for the works, based on which they offered £46,600.

We reviewed the scope of works prepared and it was clear that this was not sufficient and that it was not reasonable, given the costs of the original build. Our client wanted to do the work himself and we were able to renegotiate a settlement to include the balance of his alternative accommodation and the building costs, so that he had the freedom to do the work as and when he chose. Our client was delighted with the lump sum we agreed, instead of being forced to use insurers' contractors or accept a far lesser sum.

Case 2
We settled at £5,814 after our client's claim was initially rejected out of hand.

We were recommended to our client when insurers told him his property had not suffered water damage and that his boiler had failed due to wear and tear.

We met with our client, who owned a lovely cottage in a beautiful rural location and was clearly a good, honest, upright citizen. He had suffered water damage to his property when his central heating pipes had been leaking within the concrete floor. We met at his home, reviewed the policy wording and presented our technical arguments to his insurers. After around 2 months of correspondence, his insurers did a 180-degree about-turn and accepted the claim in full, AND offered an apology for "the delay in reaching this decision". Full payment was received within a week.

Case 3
We agreed settlement at £10,500 after insurers declined claim for storm damage.

Our client is a well-established school of further education. On Christmas Eve 2013, severe storms blew the flat roof off the main building and caused internal water damage too. The insurance company's loss adjuster – who incidentally attended but didn't bother to inspect the roof – declined the claim on the basis that the roof was old and suffering from wear and tear. They appointed a surveyor/contractor who did eventually take a look at the roof but only AFTER temporary emergency repairs had been carried out by our client.

We were appointed after the claim was initially rejected. We then actually bothered to get up on the roof and inspect it. We also reviewed all the historic data and weather records and were able to destroy the insurer's arguments and succeeded in agreeing a cash settlement of £10,500 for our client. With this sum they could repair the storm damaged roof at their own chosen time, so as not to disrupt student term time.

Case 4
Insurer offered £81,668 but we settled at £96,000, following storm/water damage to stunning high net worth property on golf course.

Our clients were a high flying family with worldwide business interests. Their stunning and unique home was severely flooded during storms when a sump pump failed and water backed up into their basement and indoor sunken pool. Following a formal tender process we agreed the scope of works, but the insurers wanted to settle based on the lowest tender. This was not acceptable to our client, who wished to use their own contractors. Even though these preferred contractors were more expensive, we managed to negotiate a compromise solution on a cash basis, so that our client could use this money for more extensive refurbishments to their home.

Case 5
Settlement and compensation agreed at £20,000 after insurers reject claim for storm damage.

Our client is a well-established accountancy practise in north London as well as the owner of a property portfolio. Their office building was badly damaged following storm damage. However, following a visit from the insurance company's loss adjuster, the insurance company then did nothing for months and indeed ultimately declined the claim without any valid reason.

Following our instruction, we analysed their decision and rebutted all their arguments. The insurers appointed a 'Dispute Resolution' firm and we met them to discuss the case. Following the meeting it was clear that the insurers were wholly wrong and they agreed to settle at around £20,000 PLUS they made a payment by way of compensation to my client.

Case 6
£14,500 agreed for accidental damage to patio doors after insurer's loss adjusters refused to pay a penny.

In this case our client's unique, architecturally designed home suffered damage when the specially built double glazed patio doors were accidentally damaged. Insurers declined the claim, arguing that they had not been "accidentally" damaged within the terms of the policy. Following our instruction, we successfully argued to the contrary, which ensured a full settlement and obtained an apology for our client!

Case 7
£9,500 agreed for water damage to a flat after insurers refused to pay loss of rent.

Our client was a well-respected former MP with a property in Westminster. When the flat suffered water damage, a claim was made for the repairs and for loss of rent, as the tenants were forced to move out. Insurers said the quotes for repair were too much and that they would not pay any loss of rent. We obtained full agreement for the repair quotes and also secured two months loss of rent, to the delight of our client.

Case 8
The FOS upholds complaint on behalf of our client who suffered storm damage to his house. Claim settled for £5500 in full after insurers rejected it for months.

Our client was renting a family home in Borehamwood, Herts. During the prolonged storms of winter 2013/2014, rainwater found its way into the house by saturating the outside wall. Insurers declined the claim on the basis that the damage was not storm related but due to lack of maintenance over a period of time. We made a formal complaint to the insurers but they stubbornly held their ground. So we took our case to the ombudsman who found in our client's favour. He was awarded the full costs of the claim and interest.

Case 9

Settlement agreed for £16,000 after insurers initially declined any payment.

In similar circumstances to case 8 above, the insurance company's loss adjuster made little effort to understand the true cause of the rot and damage to our client's living room floor. They refused to deal with the claim and after several months of poor service, we were recommended and instructed. We were able to demonstrate clearly that the cause of the damage was a leak from a pipe that our client could not reasonably have known about. The claim was not only settled eventually, but the insurer also made an ex-gratia payment along with an apology.

Case 10

We agreed settlement on a theft claim for £11,000 after the insurer originally refused to accept it.

Our clients were away on holiday when intruders broke in and stole family heirlooms and sentimental jewellery. Insurers took the view that our client had failed to disclose previous claims when asked on the proposal form. We successfully argued that these previous claims did not have to be disclosed. Insurers then tried to say that they would deal with the claim by replacing all jewellery via their suppliers. We successfully argued that the jewellery could not in fact be replaced. After they incorrectly tried to apply policy limits, we were able to secure a full cash settlement for our happy clients.

About the Author

Steve Lazarus has dealt with property damage insurance claims for 25 years. He started working for and on behalf of insurance companies as a loss adjuster, but after 15 years became disillusioned with the way the consumer was being treated and with the huge volume of complaints he ended up having to deal with on a daily basis due to poor service and poor decisions.

He set up The Claims Desk in 2004 and his practise has gone from strength to strength. He acts for a wide variety of clients, from property owners and commercial landlords to managing agents and insurance brokers, and is often sought out to provide advice on contentious claims.

Steve grew up in north London, where he has lived and worked all his life and still practices today. He went to school at Haberdashers' Aske's Boys' School and went on to obtain his law degree in Manchester. Following around three years in the property/estate agency market he entered the field of loss adjusting and property claims, where he has worked ever since.

Steve has been very happily married to the wonderful Suzanne for over 27 years and has two amazing children, David and Rosie.

Credentials and qualifications

- Has been dealing with property claims for 25 years
- Has a Law and Politics degree from Manchester Polytechnic LLb (Hons)
- Is a Chartered Insurance Practitioner
- Is an Associate of the Chartered Institute of Insurers – ACII
- Is a member of the Chartered Institute of Loss Adjusters – CILA
- Is a member of the Faculty of Claims
- Is authorised and regulated by the Financial Conduct Authority
- Posts regularly on his Facebook page (*facebook.com/Theclaimsdesk*), Google+ community (Disasters in the Home), Twitter (*twitter.com/TheClaimsDesk*), LinkedIn (*uk.linkedin.com/in/stevelazarus2*) and other social media
- Has exhibited, presented and debated at the Flood Defence and Prevention Expo 2015
- Runs a regular business networking group
- Member of The Federation of Small Businesses
- Invited to co-author book 'The Ultimate Success Secret' with Dan Kennedy

Please refer a friend to receive our free newsletter

If you are reading this book you probably receive our monthly newsletter – if not, please call us and we will sign you up.

You can enable access to this newsletter to all of your friends. Then they too can know how best to deal with insurance company denial and procrastinations, and find specific steps they can take to find the best loss assessor for their claim.

Simply scan or photograph a copy of the form opposite, fill it out and email it to *info@theclaimsdesk.co.uk* or fax it back to us on 0208 906 0063 or post it to Steve Lazarus, The Claims Desk, Phoenix House, 5 Birkbeck Road, Mill Hill, London, NW7 4BP.

Alternatively, why not send us a list of names and we will send them our newsletter, along with a note telling them that YOU HAVE HELPED to make it available to them.

We will not spam them, so if they don't wish to receive the newsletter they can simply unsubscribe and be removed from the list.

Please start a subscription to The Claims Desk FREE insurance claims newsletter for this person:

Name _____

Address _____

_____

City _____   Postcode _____

Email address _____

Referrer's name (optional) _____

Acknowledgements

People who inspired me, encouraged and supported me through the writing of this book:

Mark Beaumont-Thomas: *www.lexiconmarketing.co.uk* for editing, cajoling, correcting grammar and keeping me on track.

Paul Williams: *www.extrabold.design* for brilliant cover design, artwork and page setting.

Dan Kennedy: *www.gkic.com* for inspiring me to change the way I think about business and marketing.

Brad Burton: *www.bradburton.biz* for suggesting I use Mark and Paul in the first place.

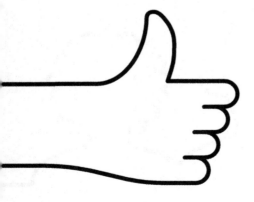

CPSIA information can be obtained
at www.ICGtesting.com
Printed in the USA
LVOW03s1557120717
541118LV00017B/1070/P